CW00865952

Poems
from a
Marriage

DAVID TAS

For Phil

my muse
my love
my life

Contents

On Parting

Acknowledgements

Special thanks to Nick Williams for his guidance and hard work in compiling this book. I am indebted also to Charles Penny for his artwork, to Nic Beale for his helpful advice and to my family for their continuing love and support.

Preface

This is a story of a great love told through poetry.

My wife Philomena, known to everyone as Phil, was born on 16th December 1942 in the ancient town of Youghal, County Cork. One of seven children she had a happy childhood and at the age of 18 made the big decision to travel to London to train as a State Registered Nurse.

After graduation she went to Glasgow to study midwifery and there we met at a party in the nurses' quarters. It was love at first sight and we were inseparable for the next 49 years until her death on 25th September 2013.

The diagnosis of Lymphoma in 1998 followed by 15 years of treatment and care at The Royal Marsden Hospital strengthened our relationship even more.

I had written poetry from an early age and the strength and fulfilment of our marriage provided the perfect environment for further efforts. This book follows the poems and prose through our lives and could not have been written without the influence of Phil's deep love, encouragement and support throughout the years.

Early Poems

Quinta *

The cottage lay upon the shore
Drenched by the breath of salt sea spray
And the child that lay in the cot asleep
Was lulled by the roll of the restless deep.

The surge of a wave would rush and roar
Followed then by a longdrawn sigh
The child stirred and a little moan
Mirrored the mystery of the advancing foam.

The child is grown, the cottage gone
The deep green sea goes on and on
Now in the night my heart is aching
For childhood's waves at Quinta breaking.

---

* Quinta was a pretty thatched cottage at Bonchurch, Isle of Wight, where I was taken as a small child on holiday.

Steyning Grammar School 1953-1959

P.C Coltman (Percy in the staff room)
taught me all he knew of English Lang.
and Lit., sparking off in my ignorant brain
a thirst and affinity for words
that make up this noble language of ours
which is insatiable until such time,
a rare event, when the rhythm
and meaning flow together in a living stream
wending its tortuous way down to a sea
that laps constantly in my mind
seeking forever true constancy in sound
and meaning.

These words, these words, honed into place
living pieces in the jigsaw of language
each has its position for a time
and yet the slightest movement, juxtaposition,
nuance, will throw everything into confusion
commencing the next search for a stone
that will provide foundation for my
thoughts and there may one build such
a castle of words and battlements with
sufficient strength and mortared meaning
that will withstand the weary winds of time
in perpetuity.

Lindfield High Street

One day I played at the start of the war
With my Hornby train set on my Granny's floor
When a strange sound suddenly came from afar
Through the front door that was always ajar.

The sound grew louder as I ran out to the street
And my heart kept time to the drum's solemn beat
As there round the bend where the gravestones lie
Came the Highland tartans with their pipes held high.

And there by The Tiger, formerly an inn,
They started to play the tune By Loch Linnhe
My heart was bursting with youthful pride
As I marched and I marched at the soldiers' side.

Past Araminta's where Granny took tea
Past the sweet smell of the old bakery
Down to the pond where the swans took fright
And on through the common in the bright sunlight.

There I left them with a tear in my eye
For the sound of the pipes make strong men cry
As they go into battle with the drum's solemn beat
And the cries of the fallen in the dust, blood and heat.

Now many years on I think of their fate
As the pipes played them in to the beaches of hate
And I march down the street to the solemn beat
Of a single drum in the noonday heat.

In Winter

A gale is roaring from the West
Enraged grey clouds storm low across the sky
All fields and woods seem filled, unblest
And branches wrested from a swaying elm
For crazy moments upwards fly.

Cold rain cuts down, cascades from roofs
Is caught by gusts of wind and rains again
The wind's alive, a thundering of hoofs
Or moaning like a tortured wraith in vain
Forever seeking, unfulfilled.

Seagulls are blown away inland
Away from their accustomed, restless deeps
To other greens on which they awkward stand
Impulsively some rise and screaming sweep
Aloft to joust with unknown gods.

Tumultuous sound, the storm has reached its peak
The air is tautly filled with thund'rous noise
Crescendoes break and then let gentler breezes seek
To scatter far and wide the lingering mists
And distant hills are seen again.

Sunday Afternoons

High on the hill stood the King Edward sanatorium
Amidst the pine trees spicing the air with resin,
Air so fresh and clear and scented with
The roses that distracted your eye
From the view to the valley below.

The marbled hall was cool and quiet
And here my mother would sit until I came
To disturb the genteel tranquillity
With oily hands from my failing Francis Barnett
And a grubby white motorcycle hat.

We would leave the murmured conversations
Over punctuated by consumptive coughs
To take short steps onto the lawns
With frequent rests while her lungs
Fought to keep up with her mind.

Tea in the overwhite room
Was welcome but neither of us
For different reasons ever remembered
The content, wherever I looked my
Eyes always came back to rest on the spittoon.

At parting she would summon up a smile
From among too many pillows
Then sink back in pallid exhaustion
Too tired to hear me vent my anger
By riding, throttle roaring, too fast down the hill.

Lindfield Fair

Always in August the fair would come
Rattling down the High Street all day long
And in every house a curtain twitched
As the village pretended nothing was wrong
For the fairfolk were not the same
They would shout and curse as they came
And all was quiet when they were gone.

Saturday was the day for setting up
The stalls and rides for the opening night
And the village green was out of bounds
As the ropes were pulled with all their might
And hammers swung with terrible force
With a rhythmic chant both loud and coarse
That gave many a child a fearsome fright.

At last, at last the evening came
And the sun sank down in the gathering gloom
To be reborn on the clouds above
Cast up by the light of the fairground fume
And then we went down the dear old High
Our eyes transfixed by the brilliant sky
Our hearts in time with the engines' boom.

Past the caravans circled around
Across the common to the noise and light
Into the smell and bustling crowd
When all around was sheer delight

The strongest man, the smallest flea
Which would provide the greater glee?
Where was the most extraordinary sight?
Who would match the boxing champ?
Or show their strength and ring the bell
Ride the switchback and see the world
As they clung on tight with many a yell
In this magic place where all was bright
Where fairground folk could banish the night
And bring village people under their spell.

A toffee apple was a bribe for home
Past the pond where the fights would be
As the night wore on and the rides ran down
With steam exhaled which we would see
As a final puff of dragon's smoke
Where the mighty beast lay down its yoke
And slumbered deep with the circus flea.

In the morning we would silently go
And walk the common with critical gaze
Where an island of bumper cars quietly marooned
On a lake of steel appeared through the haze
And behind the canvas fair dogs slept
As the world's largest lady quietly wept
At the thought of a life of fairground days.

Sunbeams

I stood in the church with my mother
Just at the end of the war
The jumble of words meant nothing
But the sunlight streamed in by the door.

The beams were broken by branches
The soldiers were living no more
But their spirits came flickering to me
There in the light on the floor.

Now mother has gone to be with them
I seek those sunbeams so gay
But I find them hard to recapture
Though I bend on my knee and I pray.

Perhaps I never shall know them
'Til the church door's left open one day
And I am carried through with the sunlight
To play on the floor while you pray.

Bognor Bank Holiday

My pace quickened as we neared the sea
The sky grew brighter reflecting
The harsh glitter of the sun
In the dash of the breaking waves.

The distant murmur began to crystallize
Became more distinct and harsher
Reaching inside you with a palpitation
Of sea cold screams and sandcastle dreams.

I lay on the pleasure pain shingle
And thoughts swum lazily by
Corpuscular goldfish in the searing orange
World that dwells behind suntaut eyelids.

Then the languid walk home along
Streets of burning tarmac with oasis trees
Providing scant shade for cooking cars
And less for long brown legs strolling in their windows.

The Lancashire family in the flat below
Were frying onions as the sun sank slowly
Down to hiss in the frying pan sea releasing
The balmy aromas of a summer's night.

Whispering tamarisks took up the scents
Caressing the fading sky with tender branches
Enveloping the warm kiosk where deep brown coins
Would conjure up the colour of her eyes before I heard her voice.

Southdown

I lay on the turf high up on the down
Mesmerized by the summer sky
Problems remained below in the town
With desks and chalk and calculi.

The mischievous wind caressed my mind
With stalks of brome grass rustling together
The warmth of the sun helped me find
A brief respite from literary endeavour.

Beneath my elevated world remained the town
Diminutive boxes in sharp relief as evening shadows crept
Like a furrow across the pathway down
A giant's image shrinking with every footstep.

Wiston Springs

There where chalk meets Wealden clay
Bursts forth a spring through night and day
Quietly feeding the clearest pond
Where grows the duckweed frond on frond
Water boatmen skim along, suddenly stop
And then go on to escape the frog that hops
And dives down to depths of crystal hue
Where streaks the kingfisher's brilliant blue
And sticklebacks flash in silver streaks
To escape the predator's piercing beak
There in the evening's shimmering light
Dragonflies rainbow in glowing flight
And when the sun sinks into the Down
The evening sky with glory crowns
This precious place with golden light
And moorhens nod forth to quietly preen,
Elderly gentlemen in stockings green.

On Leaving Home

Your brother shook you by the hand
Something he had never done
And could not look into your eyes
Mummy cried as Daddy took
The new case down the narrow stair.

"C'mon now Phil, time to go."
From outside the terraced house
Your father's voice gave comfort
As the creeping light of dawn
Lit an unfamiliar day.

Goodbye to sisters two
One with a tear in her eye
The other could not reply
But would listen for your voice
At bedtime and not understand.

The little car sped quickly through
The town, past fishing boats swinging
With the tide and the convent school
Awaiting you no more, then Perks
Amusements strangely quiet and still.

The Cork road was now a threat
For past Midleton and Killeagh
Lay the channel ferry
Instead of bustling Patrick Street
And Mummy knowing the shops.

Your father carried the case to the water's edge
And watched you struggle up a gangplank's eternity
To ironclad separation, he was still there
An aching arm forgotten in salute
As the sea irrevocably widened your life.

Love Game

"Truth, dare or promise?"
Asks the girl I love
How am I to choose
And win this mortal dove?

Truth and I must wear
My heart upon my sleeve
Dare and be so brave
Or perhaps for ever grieve.

Promise and I may know
The path I ought to take
I hope she asks a promise
A promise for true love's sake.

Breakfasts

The breakfasts were the confirmation of our love
The extension of those precious hours we spent together
Into another day.

It was a long, long time to the next evening
So many hours to the next meeting
When we would play.

The chequered cloth, the table laid for two
The early morning renewal of our love
So much to say.

The days were then much shorter
The morning taste of your sweet lips
Helped me on my way.

Now we are together, you and I
It's the breakfasts I remember, the start
To a lifetime's days.

Christmas Eve – Glasgow 1965

In my lifetime there was one Christmas Eve that stood out in memory above all others. It is probably because the particular turn of events on that evening related to a great happiness, a great joy, a feeling of closeness to something that happened two thousand years before.

I was in Glasgow on the Christmas Eve in question. It was a cold clear night with a North wind chasing the litter through the streets and prying with icy fingers into the most sheltered corners. My fiancée had a few precious hours' leave from her nursing duties, so wrapping up against the wind and leaning into its blustering face we walked away from the hospital to a roadside inn.

Inside, the warmth and Christmas decorations provided a glittering fairyland far removed from a bleak and drafty stable that was the gathering place so long ago. We talked and laughed as lovers do until all too soon it was time to leave and reluctantly we made our way from the comfortable scene expecting to struggle back through the painful blackness of the night.

The light from the door shone on a world transformed to dazzling white. The snow was falling quietly and gently wrapping the harsh city in swaddling clothes. Clean, pure, soft, rounded with no shadows, no corners just as it might have been for the coming of the Saviour.

The journey back was joyous. The words kept tumbling through my mind, "The Angel of the Lord came down and glory shone around". Our steps were light. We felt close to each other, close to Him, close to all that lived and breathed on that memorable Christmas Eve.

The Marriage Years

9th July 1966

I take thee Philomena to be my wedded wife,
to have and to hold, from this day forward,
for better, for worse, for richer, for poorer
in sickness and in health, 'til death us do part;
and thereto I plight thee my troth.

With this ring I thee wed;
this gold and silver I thee give;
with my body I thee worship;
and with all my worldly goods
I thee endow.

The Wedding Day

With this ring I thee wed
Now kneel you down and pray
That this bond shall not be shed
Within our mortal day.

Let the circle of the ring
Guide us on our joyful path
Together each the other bring
Past obstacle and pit and wrath.

Forward partner help me go
And I the same for you
Let me always feel and know
That we were ever true.

And if I weaken now and then
Turn to me and say
Your love is there to give me strength
And help us on our way.

Take my hand in your soft palm
Sooth my cares away
Give me that pervading calm
That ends the perfect day.

Honeymoon Legs

The wedding over we made our way
Down to the ferry that warm summer's day
The photograph taken on the deck so bright
Shows a woman in a halo of light
Her clothes prepared for going away
Frames a smile that will always stay
In my mind.

The steam train smoked along the track
Our suitcase carefully placed on the rack
The label looked strange as it moved in the draught
The 'Mr and Mrs' made us both laugh
For separate lives were joined into one
And if there are tears there will also be fun
In the years to come.

We emerged from the tunnel above the bay
In the fading light of a long, long day
The taxi came quickly, the hotel was near
The receptionist kind, "Your room is here,
There's a view of the sea and a cold collation"
And surely later some celebration
Of the life to be.

Thoughts stay in my mind of the days ahead
As she graced the pond wall with honeymoon legs
And exposed her body to the warm sea air
In the latest bikini, chosen with care
And secure on her finger was the golden ring
That had sealed the knot on everything
For a lifetime together.

If

If I touch your fingers
Where my mind touched long ago
I will see within your shining eyes
Whether to stay or go.

If I kiss your soft, sweet lips
Then I will surely know
How your thoughts have strayed there
Helping mine to grow.

If I hold you in my arms
With the glow of love's pure light
I will keep you there my darling
For this and every night.

Valentine 1995

Oh! Full bright light you shine
On all my long-houred days
And there dispel the gloomy haze
With one quick look I am restored
And this countenance erstwhile so flawed
With sombre thoughts, transforms
To share your smile.

Wordsong

I am the writer of beautiful words
I am the wind in the rippling corn
I am clear water running in minds
Lifting the spirit when all is forlorn.

I come from the songs that were sung before
I come from the land and the sun and the sea
I come from the night and the softness of dawn
I am the calm in the mountain's lee.

Explore with me the minds of men
Explore with me the deep heart's core
Explore with me emotions, then
Sense the perfume and hunger for more.

Thoughts

Someone is walking in my mind
And I in theirs,
Can you trespass in a space that draws
Pictures from the air?
They say ignore a star to see it clear
Look back and it is gone,
So as I entertain you in my mind
Adventure me elsewhere
And if I have equal privilege with you my friend
Walk on, walk on.

Molecule Me

I wish I were the air
And lived my life everywhere
All at once.

Embrace the ones I love
Every contour within a glove
Of me.

Dwell in all those happy places
Enfold with remembered warm embraces
Continually.

The ecstasy would burst my heart
And each millionth tiny part
Would keep me free
To wander on for ever and a day
A hovering gull in thermal play
Around the world.

Brahm's Requiem – Ardingly College

Seated in the chapel choir
The music and the words are so beautiful
They lift us up to the high places
Of our lives and in another passage
Take us to despair and mortality.

As the requiem proceeds in majesty
To the inevitable end our hands
Are clasped in love and friendship
Sealed by the years that are between us.

The slow descent into silence
Brings in its echoes the comfort of peace.

Annie Holman *

She was born in the village of Ardingly
Beneath the fleecy Sussex sky
And the deepest eyes of darkest brown
Reflected first her mother's frown
When she noticed the shoulders hunched a bit
And the tiny bones that did not fit
For Annie's back was not quite straight
So a crooked stance was to be her fate.

She grew into a cheerful child
With a Sussex accent soft and mild
A tinkling laugh and a ready smile
That hovered close by all the while
And her mother sometimes feeling sad
Knew she really should be glad
To be blessed with a child so full of grace
Though a tear still trickled down her face.

Quickly schooldays passed away
And work was the order of the day
For the little cottage was a humble home
And nothing was reaped that was not sown
So Annie learnt to stitch and sew
And on her cycle to work would go
Four miles there and four miles back
Only on Sunday could she escape the rack.

---

* Annie was a seamstress who worked for my grandmother in Lindfield, Sussex -
my mother's birthplace. She made clothes for us all.

Dresses fine for the Royal Courts
Trousers for a small boy still in shorts
Her skills produced the finest clothes
Even in winter when the bitter snows
Froze her delicate feet and hands
Making it hard to sew hat bands
And the journey home was a weary struggle
Before at the hearth she could thaw and snuggle.

Later her mother became unwell
And extra work to Annie fell
Who must work and cook and sew and clean
Did she sometimes dressmake and dream
Of a life elsewhere from Ardingly
An easier place under the Sussex sky
Where people did not work all day
But found some time to holiday?

In later years I called again
And was welcomed with that soft refrain
And the deep brown eyes and the ready smile
That had stayed in my mind all the while
Since I wore the shorts so carefully made
By a small, bent lady who will never fade
From my mind as the years creep slowly on
And the one great sadness is that she is gone.

Valentine 1998

Oh! Sweet lady how you stroll
Through all my daylight hours
And then at night's fall in scented flowers
I am remembered of your sweet lips.

So bright moon rises and soft
I hear the rustle of your dress
Murmuring in my heart and stilted breath
Foretelling the joy of your caress.

Spring in Brandon *

The East wind is blowing
And the salt sea surf
Breaking once more
In my mind
Where the Spring flowers on field banks
Dance the birth cycle
Into another year.

New lambs bleating
On the mountainside
And furze the colour
Of tiger's eyes
Bring me back to that haven
Of peace where the warmth
In those I love
Is constant as the years.

---

* We spent many holidays here with Phil's sister on the north side of the Dingle
Peninsula in County Kerry, Eire.

The Salmon Fishers of Brandon

A brave morning broke on Brandon Bay
Where salmon play in the Atlantic spray
And sea boot legs dressed in black
Carried the currach down over the wrack
To the cold and shining sea.

Can you hear the swish as the oars bite deep?
Could you hear the hiss of the greying sleet?
As the glistening craft fights her way
Out through the depths of Brandon Bay
Out to the shoals for another day.

Few words spoken in the gathering wind
Although a man might ponder if he had sinned
The oars creak loud as the nets are cast
And round in a circle the trap made fast
For the silver kings of the sea.

Haul away boys, haul away
Break your backs in the icy spray
There! Your reward will leave the deep
And silver scales through the winter keep
You warm and feed your hearth.

There at night when the black sea roars
And splintered light from the pole star soars
When the wind howls in the chimney piece
And it seems the storm will never cease
Think of those the sea has claimed.

For you brave boys must go out each day
Where the salmon swarm and flash and play
Yet the mighty ocean will claim her due
And fishing wives will weep and rue
The penance they must pay.

Brandon

I will return there where the river meets the sea
And sunshine falls in dappled showers on the far off Maharees
There where children's laughter is part of every day
And the mackerel dart and glister in the salt sea spray.

I will return there to the mountain mist again
And Slea Head standing firm in the driving wind and rain
And there may cut turf from the ancient bog so high
Where there is no sound but the seagull's plaintive cry.

I will return there to the mountains cold and grey
And I may seek peace there, the peace of yesterday
And then remember surely how my heart was ever bright
As we stood above the bay in the pale moonlight.

The Hill

I fell asleep by Brandon Bay
When the wind began to roar
And a thousand folk passed this way
Who had passed this way before.

And as each face came to mind
I knew that each belonged
Their lives and mine were intertwined
Through laughter love and song.

The long hard road that man must walk
Before the hill is won
Is scattered with black hooded crows
Each one injustice done.

So when I woke to the rising sun
And the crows had disappeared
I knew the hill could now be won
And the way ahead not be feared.

Valentine 1999

There is a lady fair and true
Who took my heart through eyes of blue
And in her gaze of sparkling light
Shone a future full and bright
That still remains year on year
Though cast sometime with solemn tear
And yet through any mist that's cast
I know true love will serve and last
So in this joyful bond we share
Rest safe my sweet in love's true care.

Near Madrid *

One day near Madrid
In the high desert
In the heat of the morning sun
A hummingbird hovered
Over her bright clothing
Seeking nectar where there was but cloth
Bright cloth of flowers
Over a heart that emphasised
With the pulsating wings
Two hearts, two creatures
Juxtaposed for that brief moment
In one searing world of heat and light
So bright I had to turn away
With tears of joy.

---

* We spent a holiday with a nephew in Madrid, New Mexico.

New Mexico

The mesa is a quiet, hot limb of the desert
On which stands a lonely house solitary as a cloud
In the New Mexican sky.

The way to the house is long and tortuous
The thread of life sucked through gnarled roots
By juniper and pine.

Here the earth is ruled by the burning sun
Giving way to none other than elemental fire and water
Or firmament of night.

Here I have known the quietness of the soul
That broods in the silence of the desert
Among old bleached bones.

And yet as twilight falls a rustling wind
Springs from nowhere, stirring the solitude into sound
That brings hope.

The lamp must be lit to shine forth on barren wastes
Of lonely desert, pleading my thoughts into the night
Awaiting your return.

Lamplight

A lamp hangs on the kitchen wall
'Farms Lamplight' all the way
From New Mexico.

It hung in the old adobe house
Where the bear came at night
Looking for food.

The bear destroyed everything
With mighty paws in his search
But mistrusted the paraffin.

The lamp now burns in our kitchen
Against the night and dreams
Of darker times.

So we sit and talk and eat
In the comforting light
Of evolution.

The Lizard

The lizard clings to the sun-drenched wall
Warming its blood in the hottest rays
With eyes deep, black and motionless
Encompassing all with a reptilian gaze.

Black and yellow run nose to tail
In shimmering streaks of reflected light
Drawn from treasures buried deep
Jet and gold, so pure, so bright.

A simple creature to all our eyes
Rustling dry from place to place
Yet when all around is war and shout
This jewel will outlast the human race.

Valentine 2000

On this day and those gone by
I may be found lingering
In some quiet spot
Where I know my true love
Passes by.

And as the time approaches
My heart's beat will sing
Like butterflies' wings
Palpitating
On high.

So here my lady comes
With lightsome step and graceful air
And as I step into her path
To hear her merry laugh
So love will ne'er die.

Trees

Slow to grow and slow to die
Tall trees fill the towering sky
The oak, the ash, the sycamore
Shade the mighty forest floor.

Reaching up in supplication
Creaking arms bear foliation
Green and winsome in the summer
Shading glades for happy lovers.

Winter's gales strip off the leaves
Yet leave little time to grieve
Before the buds that silent wait
Bring forth the spring in rushing spate.

Then the world is full of glory
Flowers and ferns repeat the story
Gently filling nature's store
Life is bursting forth once more.

Morning Milking *

Wash down the parlour and set the machines
Then off down the track where the early mist
Levels the valley into glacial white
Pierced only by stranded mountaintop trees.

"C'mon! C'mon!" echoes my cry
As the gate draws near with Phillipa waiting
To lead them in, flanks warm to the touch
And grating hooves on trackbed flints setting my teeth.

Steaming in the yard they wait patiently
To join the daily symbiosis
Of crushed barley and a gentle hand
Traded for rich milk gurgling over the cooler.

The churns are filled one by one and as cows meander
Back to the pasture I dip the ladle
Into the frothing milk, filling the can
To consummate the morning's work at breakfast time.

---

* I was a farm manager in Sussex for many years.

The Spring

In the spring I breathe again
No more the winter's shallow pang
But deeply, surging, easing pain
Restoring faith and then I can
Take up the mock of human lie
And gaze beyond the blue, blue sky.

Beyond, beyond to other minds
Sprung out of our eye's compass
By green buds bursting that unwind
Our very pith and end the fast
At last, at last let's sing
The coming of the spring.

Hoeing the Beet

The labourers creep across the field
In a staggered line between the rows
Thinning the plants to produce the yield
That comes from the rhythm of their hoes.

The field is vast and stretches far
Across the rich fens peaty land
And in the distance Boston Spa
Shimmers, an oasis in the sand.

The noonday sun is mounting high
Above the aching backs beneath
Yet every time the headland's nigh
The cant completed brings relief.

And as the sun slows to the West
A skylark sings high and clear
The labourers pause to take a breath
Knowing day's end is once more near.

Valentine 2001

Go soft sweet heart into that brighter sun
That kisses eyes and cheeks and golden hair
With warmth and tenderness of balmy winds
Which, mischievous with perfumes rare
Caress your soul on such high days as these
Then, when in some quiet moment there
You may think of me across a turquoise sea
Know well your thoughts are halfway met
By those I send from this cold shore
And burning bright where'er they meet
Will shine that precious beacon to guide you home again.

The Shepherd

The high down sees the shepherd stride
Into the teeth of a blustering gale
The sheep are scattered far and wide
From windblown ridge to sheltered vale.

A piecing gaze that sweeps the hill
From beneath a dripping, broad-brimmed hat
Seeks the lamb that has taken ill
Searches the ewe that is on her back.

A shadow feathers at his heels
Wet nose brushing the flying smock
To every whistle away it wheels
Forever circling within the flock.

He must by now be wet and tired
Striding on through the spreading storm
Lucky the man who has him hired
Counting his blessings inside in the warm.

Seasons

Morning sun lift my heart
Warm my body in gentle part
Bring new hope to every day
Through the blooming of the May
Green the buds that are bursting now
Overseeing the trusty plough
Stroking seed into the land
From the labourer's steady hand.

There in soil's warming womb
Sprout the seeds up through the gloom
Seeking light and air and rain
Giving the land her cloak again
Green the mantle that slowly grows
Marching the fields in ordered rows
'Til the harvest comes once more
Filling with gold the farmer's store.

Soon the days will shorter be
And leaves fall soft from every tree
There the warmth will now be lost
With the coming of the frost
And winter wind pries the land
Chaffing sore the farmer's hand
That splits the log to feed the fires
As snow falls cold on churches' spires.

Now is the time to sit and dream
In fire's light of all that's been
And savour slow past summer's light
In the bleak midwinter night
Think of laughter 'midst the hay
When all around was bright and gay
Winter now will soon be spring
And church bells once more merry ring.

The Month of May

As I breathe my breath
And enter one more month of May
I give thanks for the wealth
Of beauty all around me
And the brightness of the day.

For every year that passes by
The spring brings hope anew
The birds that shimmer on the wing
Glorify the clouds above
Floating upon a sea of blue.

The hawthorn blooms the purest white
Among the greening fields
And skylarks sing above the hills
Lifting up my spirit high
To church bells' glorious peals.

This spring is one I treasure above
Those that have gone before
For the years are passing one by one
And the falling mist of the lime tree flowers
Is clouding that which lies in store.

For Luci's Birthday *

Go forth softly into each birth year
Listen carefully for birdsong
And sense the breathy perfume of a rose
Be not afraid of peace or
Those quiet times at the setting of the sun
And the rising of the moon
When islands of tranquillity will
Bring you thoughts of those you love
And through such pools of happiness
We will ever remember your smile.

* Our daughter Luci.

Valentine 2002

Here is a gift on Valentine's Day
And in a portrait gently framed
Your sweet visage with sparkling eye
And bosom soft and pale, which
Reflected in my eye and longing gaze
Brings back such joy to me
I would seek more of this kind
And gifting you such treasures everyday
Would revel in your reflected beauty
'Til I could take no more
Then like an eagle sated on his prey
Rest awhile before taking wing

Then could my lady truly say
This love hath no measure, night or day.

In Summer

Tranquillity flows through a summer afternoon
Torpor infusing all thought with languid streams
Of delicious meanderings, gently caressing banks
That sigh heavy with the scent of sagging blooms.

Willowing trees arrest gently passing notions
Stroking them softly as they turn slowly to and fro
Each tendril exploring their surge and fall
So no surface or cranny is left unmoved.

Tantalising nebulae drift in and out of view
Precursors to fusion of thoughts sublime
Held firmly between undulating walls
That have spawned the world since the birth of time.

Impulses rise and swell through tactile waves
Shaping the slowly passing hours with loving care
Into longdrawn circles rippling ever outwards
Unbroken musings of a summer's afternoon.

A Letter from a Father to his Daughters

It seems a long time ago that you arrived and I do not think I have ever consciously given any thought to the fact that one day you would no longer be here all or even most of the time.

That day has come.

It arrived in a stealthy way, quietly but inevitably creeping nearer until suddenly it pounced and in the pouncing was a glorious departure to new horizons and after that momentous spring a silence and the stillness of deep water moving inexorably through the time-worn channels of experience.

These twenty years or more have seen laughter and tears, pleasure and pain, success and failure but through these experiences the bonding has taken place that can only be expressed in one word – love. Love for each other, love for others, love for the world, love for life and if I have helped to leave anything in your hearts it must be this one feeling from which all else flows.

Faith will help you stay the path, hope will lift you in adversity, charity will open your heart but love is the core of humanity for without it all must shrivel and die.

My children, now my friends, we will meet from time to time and in each and every place will be a celebration of happiness for you have love in your hearts as I in mine.

Your ever loving father.

The Labourer

The labourer is now retired
But work is part of life
He stalks the roadside verges now
Where drains are blocked and weeds are rife.

The tools he used throughout the years
Are always close beside
The sickle sharpened like a spear
The spade that is his pride.

The midday sun is fiercely hot
As he cuts the verge so neat
Completely happy with his lot
Unperturbed by the searing heat.

The rhythmic clink of spade on stone
Matches the thrush that cracks the snail
He knows full well he is not alone,
Savours the life throughout the vale.

The sun falls slowly through the sky
The long day's work is nearly done
Home is calling and evening nigh
One more thread of life is spun.

The Evergreen Oak

There is an oak that I pass by
Broad and green beneath the sky
Spreading wide a sturdy frame
Offering shade to those who came
To climb the hill above.

This oak is clothed throughout the year
Stable when any mortals fear
The summer heat or winter blast
There they may always seek repast
From a traveller's fatigue.

I passed that oak when I was young
When everyday had a brighter sun
When every leaf was a field of green
And every girl was a fairy queen
To fill my heart with joy.

It gives me greater pleasure now
To gaze from beneath a furrowed brow
At a lifelong friend who has not changed
And will always be there as arranged
When I want to go.

Alicante to Barcelona (Saint Saens)

The express is leaving for Barcelona
At twenty three hundred and seventeen
But the difference tonight is my daughter
And friend who travel though still in their teens.

They both have their packs and their youth
To carry them on through the night
No seats are reserved and nothing to drink
Which we would demand as of right.

The longest journey has started
With places assured from their birth
We can watch and offer our guidance
As they enter the breaking surf.

We taught them to swim as the years went by
Stroke upon stroke, slowly learning the part
Now it is we who must wait their return
As the night-throbbing diesel pounds at our hearts.

For Karen *

In the early autumn mists
A child was born
When all the hedgerows' blossomed fruit
Told the world of beauty
And all around and through that birth
The beauty now was ours to hold
And love and cherish through
All the coming years

Each autumn now I look
Upon the hedgerows proud
With all their summer fruits
A rosehip there or blackberry
Glistening in the sunlit dew
And then a little smile will come
As I gaze again with admiration on
A perfect nose, eyes, lips and hair.

---

* Our daughter Karen.

Valentine 2004

Good lady thirty years are gone and more
Since I first gazed on your sweet face
And thirty springs have seen the thaw
That ends the winter's cold embrace
Now summer is not long away
When warmth and laughter have their time
And lips so soft will hold in sway
My love that flowers with columbine
All grace I wish you in summer's sun
When light will spin your flaxen hair
Into fine cloth where gold doth run
And bright shards light us everywhere

So Madam now the time has come
When I ask you as my Valentine.

The First Frost

The frost is here for a moonlit night
Has rendered every surface white
Waxing full in the October sky
The brilliant orb was slow to die
Leaving a cloth of icy crystal
On every fern and spiky thistle.

Cattle stand in moonlit shadow
Still as statues through the meadow
Ruminant dragons breathing smoke
Resting from the straining yoke
Of warmer days in dusty furrow
Nor thinking of the frozen morrow.

A hint of dawn warns the searching owl
To leave the furry creatures prowl
Through another day as golden light
Fractures frozen dewdrops bright
Warming the earth with shimmering rays
Keeping away dark winter days.

Dawn

Early morning in a frost-bound field
The ice is crunching under my feet
White and crisp the frozen grass
The earth is still, so cold, asleep.

The blood red dawn stains the sky
Pushing out from the womb of night
The flowing flesh of another day
Yawning its way into the light.

The crimson lifetide ripples out
And tops the silent, sentinel trees
Giving substance to their naked limbs
Adding colour to their shaking leaves.

The moment of silent awe is now
Before the sun blinds the searching eye
My heart is bursting in sympathy with
The life that is surging through the sky.

The Great Storm *

The heat of the October night
Was unusually intense
The fine drizzle blew every way
In the lamplight and
There was something disturbing
About its warm caress
As though a sorceress brushed
My lips with her breast
Stirring fire within by sensation
Of what was to come.

The wind was gentle at first
But unpredictable
As though it was toying with an idea
Not yet fully formed,
Restlessly turning this way and that
Seeking a solution
To the structured comfort of our lives
That would forever
Tear apart those fixed horizons
Imprinted in our minds.

---

* The hurricane of 1987.

Rustling fingers probed around the house
Whistled through trees
Gradually increasing the intensity of sound
'Til the rasping roar
Of the storm struck the land
With blow after mighty blow
Tiles flew and chimneys fell through roofs
Smashing to the ground
And the wind was King and Devil both
Crushing all around.

At last grey light crept through the land
Laying bare the battlefield
The awesome sight of limb upon twisted limb
Entangled in death
Torn from sockets of mighty trunks that lay
Heavily like straws from the threshing
Bruised and bleeding upon the ground – so
No mortal hand had struck
To change the land from that we knew
And no bird sang.

Valentine 2005

That happy hour when we first met
Lingers in my mind, and yet
Each passing day and hour and year
Brings to me a love so fair
That winter's cold and summer's heat
Are mild compared with my heart's beat
Whene'r you come with gracious smile
To speak soft words and stay awhile
Perhaps embrace or give a kiss
And turn my whole world into bliss
With perfumed breath and lingering eyes
And soft red lips that testify

No man that lacks your tender kiss
May have a love as great as this.

Land Tide

The sun was dying over the farm
As November mist came swirling round
Enveloping the yard and barn
With lingering arms that made the ground
Into a landlocked sea.

The cattle lowed with grass green tongues
As grave damp currents chilled their limbs
And sought a way through bracken fronds
Seeing their seaweed fingers spin
In earthy eddies.

Leaves no longer rustled on trees
But drowned like clammy feathers
Cast down from doves in silent eaves
Of dripping buildings, islands tethered
In the ocean's gloom.

The Fairy Ring

The winter day drew towards its close
As I tramped the sticky plough
And skirted the final quickset hedge
By an oak with naked winter bough.

My eye was drawn into the wood
To a glistening roundel of toadstools white
Encompassing a sacred circle
Guarding it with a ghostly light.

Once through the hedge a quietness fell
About my ears and made me pause,
No rabbit ran or feather rustled
The silent circle was the silence source.

Was this where Oberon and Titania lay
Within the magic fairy ring?
Which way would a weak mortal run
If a fairy voice began to sing?

Into the circle through the white surround
To become a slave of the fairy king?
And then to dance on hallowed ground
Whirling, swirling, an enchanted spin.

Or should I stumble the other way
Away in the dark and gathering gloom
Ignoring a world I believe to be there
But run from what? Away from whom?

I will stay awhile but not too long
Savouring the place where spirits gambol
And in the twilight see them play
Then lighthearted homeward ramble.

Winter

The snow comes softly in the night
Ghosting the land with an envelope white
Where soon the rays of the morning sun
Will splinter to shards of iridescent light
A million frozen snowflakes bright.

A rabbit lollops across the field
Pausing to release a smoky breath
And sniff and smell the cold, cold air
He must not stay nor tarry there
For foxes may have left their lair.

Icicles hang from building's eves
Nature's Swords of Damocles
Glistening weapons with lethal tips
Threatening all who move below
Until disarmed by sun's warmed drips.

As evening falls and darkness too
The waking owl calls "To Whit! To Whoo!"
And mice seek shelter in fear of death
For winter is cruel and its cold breath
May fall on those who stray from home.

Home where the farmer's fire burns bright
And sweet smelling woodsmoke curls in the night
Where the North wind blows and rattles the door
Where friends by the fire in warmth and ale
Will evermore tell winter's tale.

Warmth

Warmth is the contrast
I feel the most
The difference between death
And the living host
When your toes and fingers
Are numb with cold
And the North wind is searing
Through wood and wold
Then warmth is the friend
You would have on your side.

Speak out loud
In the fire's light
When the day is strangled
By the grasping night
And the awesome blizzard
Freezes the flesh
But speak with reverence
At the chimney's breast
Of the warmth you hold and now caress
For it is fickle as a lover's gentleness.

Uploders *

The Dorset hill stands high above
Solid in the early morning sun
Whose prying light casts contoured shadows
Across strip lynchetts marking man's
Ancient hard won strips of soil.

Cattle now graze where crops once grew
But still walk down the road at milking time,
The road where lengthmen broke the stone
And cut the ditch by the narrow bridge
They built with graceful arches replacing the ford.

The stream runs deep past lichened apple trees
And echoes on past oak and willow,
Flowers and ferns which line the banks
Until an open pool of sunlight
Dapples down onto a speckling trout.

The sun is higher now and in the shimmering heat
The towering oaks seem near the sky
Where a lone buzzard thermals slowly
With piercing gaze seeking a hapless rabbit
Midway between the sea and Eggardon Hill.

---

* Uploders is a village near Bridport in Dorset.

Valentine 2007

The lavender in bloom
With sweet perfume
The rose so pretty
To make her swoon
The noonday sun
As bright as gold
Will surely bring her
To my side, so I may
Once more confirm my love
And dizzy with her lips and eyes
I shall request this greatest prize
Her hand in mine

What shall she say?
Mayhap that she will love me everyday.

Christmas Eve

On Christmas Eve a daughter came
And then another, hours apart
Evening fell and lights came on
Heralding rebirth in my heart.

Those few hours once were years
Now foreshortened to an afternoon
When memories are dusted off
As grains of sand blow off a dune.

Festive days slipped quickly past
Punctuated by moments when
A glance, a look, a laugh, a smile
Would encapsulate old times again.

Then they left us one by one
For New Year's Day would soon be here
And an ageing heart could then prepare
To face with strength the coming year.

For Phil on New Year's Day

Oh! That I were a mirror bright
To gaze upon such beauty eye to eye
And in the lustrous pale moonlight
Shout with joy to the widening sky
Now should a thousand years go past
Such privilege I could not find
To ever match true love's repast
That first put you into my mind.

Prayer Flags

High in the mountain pass
Above the clouds
The many coloured prayer flags
Crack in the bitter wind
Of the glacier.

Each flag a prayer
Of different coloured words
Living contrast
To the inanimate white
Of snow and ice.

The breaking flags
Shred sentences to words
Of colour
Dancing on the wind
To the valley floor.

And there a child
Looks in wonder
As a coloured snowflake
Caresses a soul
Into her hand.

The Foreshore – Dungeness

Railway carriages
Stranded on the beach
In a broken train
Of circled wagons
With no Indians
Just the sea
Circling slowly
Around the perimeter
Seeking the breach.

Some have gardens
Of sea kale
And driftwood
In intricate patterns
Broken by snakes
Of rope woven
On rusting metal
Near old anchors
Awaiting the sea.

Incessant wind
Creates a gale
In the broken cabin
Of an old fishing vessel
Drawn up near a shack
On rotting sea legs,
Safe anchorage
For boat, house and garden
In this time.

Dreams

If I come downstairs in the middle of the night
A child that cried or an unknown sound
I feel I have crossed to the other world
Where thoughts hold sway over animate things
My mind expands to fill the void
Created from the gossamer thread
Of other people's dreams.

As I wander from room to room
Where nothing moves and nobody comes
Our precious daytime ornaments
Are reduced to pallid insignificance
Absorbed, engulfed by my night thoughts
That spit them out into a pit
Of unimportance.

I roam beyond these four stone walls
Beyond the field and the hill behind
Beyond the world, the sun, the stars
Into ethereal space where minds hold sway
And gambol outwith their earthly clay
Turning the night into a day
Of symbiotic feasting.

The succour I find on the night wind's breath
Carries me back into my flesh
Back through the rooms I so despised
Back up the stair to my wife's warm side
Who stirs and sighs for she is not there
But far outside on the currents of air
That dreamers ride.

Valentine 2010

Will you be my Valentine
'Midst the February snow?
Where all around is white and cold
And icicles of doubt freeze many a heart
While snowflakes drift to maze our minds
Such chilly thoughts need love's warm glow
As the nectaring flower seeks the honey bee
Or the cooing dove a loneing mate
And thus true love will propagate
The constancy of those who seek
In passion a long lasting kiss
In sweetness a soft bosom's bliss

So as I take your hand in mine
Will you be my Valentine?

Cancer Ward – December 2010

She is not here, the house lies quiet
Her presence felt through positioned ornaments
And photographs of all the ones she loves
I burn the advent candle every night
And feel her spirit in the brightness of the flame
As each long hour drips down the stem
And solidifies thought into reality.

As this night falls and darkness seeps into our rooms
In another place the cancer ward is harshly lit
So succour may be given with accuracy and care
And when she sleeps then I may lay awake
To watch over her sweet face and rapid breath
And hope that in the lightening of the dawn
She will return before the coming of this Christmas Day.

The Wreck of the Immacolata

Midnight and the great North wind
Is roaring into Daymer Bay
Giant waves crash onto rocks and spin
Back out to join the foaming fray.

Hard pressed and with no guiding light
A tall ship runs before the gale
Decks awash and the fearful night
Tearing apart her every sail.

Italian skies are far away
The warm blue sea a fading dream
As the Immacolata strikes Greenaway
Where the jagged rocks gape deathly green.

Warm the spices and rich the wine
Laid with care in the ship's deep hold
By dark eyed men, brown, aquiline
Who set forth on this journey bold.

A massive wave brings down the mast
The rocks are struck and the sailors' scream
Is lost in recall of all things past
As the deck explodes, seam on seam.

In the cavern of their minds
The sea now seeps with cold intent
Paralysing all it finds
Numbing forever each past event.

Out in the bay the undertow
Takes the corpses one by one
Remorselessly the deep sea flow
Passes Doom Bar where the tide must run.

Deathly white in the cold grey dawn
Lay the sailors stiff and cold
Tossed about as the green sea spawns
Its victims out then backward rolls.

Brea Hill now gazes on their graves
Where they lay in the sand three by three
St. Enedoc's spire bent to the waves
Guides their path to eternity.

Softly there her crew now sleep
Away from the wind and raging sea
Away from the storm and ocean deep
Quiet in St. Enedoc's sheltered lee.

Whitefriars Glass

The glass stands on the window ledge
Where the sunlight penetrates the depths
A curled fist, jagged knuckled, solid
Green glass, sea grass crystal clear
Therein the ocean lies
In permanent beauty forged from sand
And in the white heat turned from rock to rock.

I pick it up to the light
And see the ocean deep from shore to shore
Green turns to blue then green again
A restless tide that never stills
Reflecting the crucible that lies
Beneath the ever shifting sands
Turning the world within my hand.

Valentine 2012

Will you once more be my Valentine?
With your peacock feathers fine
Where a multitude of eyes of blue
Tell me you will always be true
And in return my love so deep
Though the path be often steep
Will bring us to that happy place
Where our everlasting warm embrace
Will carry on through life's quick run
And when all earthly things are done
We will be together evermore
In love's sweet golden store.

Exeter Cathedral

In the cathedral stood a boy
Close by his father's guiding hand
And gazed a long while at the choir
Where voices raised in praise sang high.

Patiently his father stood
Waiting absorption of light and sound
Into a mind that slowly turned
Sensation around and around and around.

The boy with a gentle turn of the shoulder
Moved to a pillar towering high
And knelt at the base to lean his cheek
Against cold stone where a man might cry.

The father gazed at the light above
Where stained glass colour misted down
And through his tears prayed so hard
That an angel's wing would soon come down
To touch his son's lifelong frown.

On Going Deaf

I cannot remember the sound of your voice
As your lips move in their sweet rhythm
Trying to penetrate the wall of water
Imitating the sea raging in my ears.

I can see the love in your eyes
That tells me sound is not everything
That the message will reach me
As you ride the surf to touch my mind.

Your gentleness will overcome the fear
Of never hearing you laugh again
And, in time, I shall learn to play
A symphony for you through my hands.

At The Royal Marsden – Bud Flanagan West Ward

We have had a cancer week
And all I want to do is sleep
Last weekend she became ill
With no breath, no energy, no will
To do her normal tasks
And so to hospital we went
Where my burden was lifted by
Doctors and nurses whose expertise
I trust implicitly.

Then slowly and step by step
They assessed and discussed
The new dragon breathing fire
Into her bloodstream.

'Haemolytic Anaemia' was his name
A monster of mutation where the blood
Feeds on itself destroying all
That enables life.

She is so brave and strong in the midst
Of canulae and drips and no sleep
And the ticking of the blood transfusion machine
That I cry when I leave at her fortitude
And my humble weakness gains strength
From those who care for her.

She sits on the bed, shoulders bare
In the prettiest of nightdresses
Marred only by the lifeblood feeding
Into the back of her hand,
Her hair swept back
In a graceful wave.

There lies the girl I married all
Those years ago and nothing has
Changed, not in her, not in me,
Not in our deep and undying love.

Her strength and beauty
Are my shining light,
The spun gold of her hair
And those eyes of blue
Give me strength to carry on
And try to ease the pain
In both our minds.

Bud Flanagan Outpatients at The Royal Marsden Hospital

The clinic in the afternoon
Is quiet and warm and comforting
The patients reclining in their chairs
Reading or sleeping with a heaviness
That weighs down eyelids in the drowsy air.

Each has an infusion pump
Measuring strong liquids to the veins
Ticking out the length of life
Staccato and at different stages
Living clocks in the horologist's shop.

At day's end each clock will stop
And patients waking from their dreams
Will shake themselves into the world
Where life's sweet pulse is now restored
With these few hours of tender care.

Coming Home

"The treatment finishes today
And tomorrow home
Or so they say
One more blood test
And if that's ok
Come and get me at midday
And don't be late!"

Tomorrow comes
I drive with joy
Anticipating her release
My love, my life
Will once more be
Home again with me.

The many corridors
Fly by, the nurses smile
Showing all is well
I peer through the window
Of her door
And there she sits expectantly
Dressed to perfection
And her golden hair
Foretelling sunshine and fresh air.

"Hello my darling."
A lingering kiss
That sweet, sweet smile
For which I have travelled
So many miles.

"Have you brought the present
And the card?
For they have been so good
Once more and I am so happy
To be going home."

They wave goodbye
And wish us well
As I take her hand
And slowly walk
Through all the doors
To the outside world
She loves so much.

Every time that we come home
The pattern stays the same
Leave the case, a cup of tea
And then into the garden
Her domain.

"How this has grown
And that one too
Those flowers so lovely
Well done you
Now I just need to tidy this
Oh! This is bliss
To be home again."

I watch as she inspects each leaf
Touching here and smelling there.
"I need a plant for this small space
Perhaps the Nursery this afternoon?"
"Don't do too much," I say
But know I'll never win
For she is in her element
And shining eyes foretell
Returning strength
Among the world she loves.

I watch from a little way
And know that on this special day
My beloved has come home
Once more
There is no more to say.

Candlelight

Light me a candle when I die
View it not with a tearful eye
The flame will flicker and then grow strong
My spirit will linger, it will not be gone.

The glow of the candlelight bathes us both
Your body, my soul in eternal troth
And every candle that you think to light
Will help us through the blackest night.

The longing you have for what we had
Will make you alternately happy and sad
The world I live in is not elsewhere
It's the tips of your fingers, the wind in your hair

You were my strength when I was alive
When I am gone you will have enough pride
From our loving and giving to carry you through
To that glorious day when our embrace we renew.

Easter Card with a Blue Gate

And in passing through the gate
We were together, looking at
A new horizon more beautiful
Than those gone by, for each gate
And each horizon was a step
Along the way together
So through the years there was a
Great peace between us, a peace
Uncommon but present here in
Friendship, respect and fortitude
Bonded by the deepest love
Against which no barrier may hold fast.

On Parting

On Parting

My maiden has fallen asleep
And the many years of loving wakefulness
Are at an end

Joined together as we always were
Hip to hip and hand to hand
She does not sleep alone

On this dull earth we parted
In her sweet heaven she started
A life apart

Her fluttering eyelids foretold death
There with that last drawn breath
It had to be

My prayers now with her constantly
In some soft place where she may lay
Until I am with her every day.

Annie's Clock

The hands that wound the clock before
No longer need the measurement of time
The hours, the days, the years gone by
Kept pace with a heart's pulsating rhyme.

Now I wind the clock each day
Five turns for chimes and five for hours
And carefully measure my life's span
As harvest reaps the blue cornflowers.

When I am gone from here anon
And clock's tick means no more to me
Reflect a moment as you wind a day
For life's short measure will quickly flee.

Youghal Bay *

Come with me to wide Youghal Bay
Where the dawn comes creeping grey
And the salmon run in the crinkling sea
And youth was spent there forever free.

Come to the strand so long, so wide
Where life goes running with the tide
Out at first for a long, long while
When every hour brought forth a smile.

Come again as the years go by
Cast back your mind with many a sigh
For the hand you held, no longer there
Nor the eyes so blue in a face so fair.

Come down now in the evening's gloom
Listen to the waves' remorseless boom
As the tide comes in across the sand
And you seek in vain the familiar hand.

---

* Pronounced 'yawl', Youghal was Phil's birthplace in County Cork, Eire

Sweet Breath of Death

A gentle breath upon my cheek from those I loved so well
Is with me still, year on year, and so I now can tell
They are here present in my mind and in the air
Each tiny particle hovering through land and oceans fair.

Through summer's heat and winter's chill a laugh I hear
Or a smile I see and when I am lonely need have no fear
For you walk through my mind with the speed of light
And banish again those long hours of blackest night.

We will fly the southern ocean, land on the silvery moon
Laugh in the rainbow, eat strawberries from a silver spoon
Go hand in hand to dance through meadows sweet
Gaze in awe once more at a tiny baby's feet.

Thank you for what you were, thank you for what you are
Go on for ever and ever being my brightest star
Lead me on through dusk and dawn each lingering day
My strength is ever knowing that you will always stay.

Family Man

The house is very quiet
I am on my own
It has happened before
But not for long
I always knew one day
The time would come
For one of us.

I am walking the rooms
Hearing sounds
Through photographs and seeing
Movement in possessions
That I am afraid to touch
Lest a lingering scent
Be released.

To sit in a favourite chair,
Not mine but one of yours
Is unbearably poignant
And moves me on in search
Of your laughter, your tears,
Your warmth, your elusive
Echoing voice.

If I can remember happiness
In your heart then
This solitude is my reward
Uplifting petty melancholy
Through the mists of time
Enabling long drawn days
To pass.

The Tide

The melting of the snow
In this first spring
Tells me you will no longer go
Your hand in mine
To face the warming sun.

For life must ebb and flow
And you have gone from me
On the flooding tide
Now I cannot hide
The tears I shed for you.

Your spirit is ever near
And each day helps me on
To tread the lonely path
That one bright day
Will bring me to your arms again.

Footprints in the Snow

As I walk the paths we walked before
With beauty all around
Her hand in mine tells me once more
That she is by my side

Laughing, talking, knowing flowers
That blossom on the way
She guides me to a special bower
Where we sat and kissed one day

She is always by my side
As Winter comes and days are slow
One thing I can never have
Her footprints in the snow.

Solace

The photographs are there
But she is gone
The ornaments and decorations
Speak volumes of her skills
And there the piece of board
She asked me to cut, not quite square
Decorated now with two brooches
And above the words in many colours
"Happiness is from Within".

Climb the stair and there
In the attic room upon the wall
A sampler painstakingly embroidered
In the long hours when she felt ill
The words resonate in my mind
"It is the purest sign
that we love someone
if we choose to spend
time idly in their
presence when we could
be doing something
more constructive".

All the years that have gone
Go on and on
For she is here
In my small sphere
Guiding me forward
With all that I do
She is holding my hand
From some other land
Where no illness or pain
Will assail her again
And one day I will rest
With my head on her breast
And we will be joined
Together again.

Ashes

There above the valley
A summer house on a high terrace
Open to the wind

We have stood in the portal
Close together, hand in hand
And wondered at the perfect view

New trees are planted now
Fresh pine, birch and Douglas fir
Growing monumentally to the sky

Now that she is gone
The noonday sun gives me
The spun gold of her hair

And in the long years to come
The soughing of the wind in high branches
Will give me the sound of her soft voice

The brilliant sky of blue
Portrays the colour of her eyes
Bringing tears to mine

Her ashes rest among the trees
As mine will sometime mingle there
Joining her once more

Then the agony of grief will end
And when the wind blows
In high branches
We will softly sing again
The songs we sang before

Fermoyle Strand

The ribbed sand glisters from the falling tide
As I walk toward the breaking surf
White water stretching far and wide
Remorselessly since nature's birth.

No longer is she by my side
Where once she stood and smiled at me
A mist of tears too strong to hide
Brings me to the restless sea.

And then I look beneath my feet
Innumerable seashells scattered there
Reflecting in the brilliant light
Her sparkling eyes, her golden hair.

Then the mist begins to clear
And I know I do not walk alone
For she is with me everywhere,
Everywhere I choose to roam.